WAY OF THE CROSS

Text by Renzo Agasso
Illustrations by Maurizio Boscolo

ST PAULS

Original title: *Via Crucis*

© 1994 Edizioni San Paolo srl, Cinisello Balsamo, Italy

Translated by D. Mary Groves OSB

Scripture texts translated by John Bligh

ST PAULS
Middlegreen, Slough SL3 6BT, United Kingdom
Moyglare Road, Maynooth, Co. Kildare, Ireland
60-70 Broughton Rd, Homebush, NSW, 2140, Australia

English language edition © 1995 ST PAULS (UK)
ISBN 085439 487 7

National Library of Australia
Card Number and ISBN 1 875570 51 9

Printed in Italy

ST PAULS is an activity of the priests and brothers of the
Society of St Paul who proclaim the Gospel through the me-
dia of social communication

Introduction

The Way of the Cross has with the Rosary characterised the religious practice of popular piety from the thirteenth century to our own day.

It has produced a kind of natural ritualising of the faith of the Christian people which from its first beginnings has celebrated the cross as the means of salvation.

The first apostolic proclamation was centred on the Passion, Resurrection and Glorification of Christ. Starting from Peter's first sermon, this evangelical nucleus is present:

'Jesus of Nazareth, this man handed over to you according to the definite plan and foreknowledge of God, you crucified and killed by the hands of those outside the law. But God raised him up, having freed him from death' (Acts 2:23-24). And Paul gives the Christians a forceful reminder (1 Cor 2:2): 'I decided to know nothing among you except Jesus Christ, and him crucified.' The

Gospels themselves take their development from the Passion and Resurrection of Christ, making it one central act in their proclamation. In particular the Gospel of Mark, so rich in details of the Passion, takes on a liturgical brevity to cover the night of Easter Eve, leading to the Resurrection celebrated with the breaking of the bread at dawn on the Sunday.

The Church has always drawn great profit and inspiration from the memorial of the Passion. *Inspiration* through free involvement of the feelings in meditating on the Passion. And prayer does also necessitate the feelings so that the whole person may be involved. *Profit* in the celebration of a salvific event. Christ saved us once and for all by dying on the cross and rising again: the facts celebrated in the sacrament of the Eucharist, the Mass. But it is just as certain that every other action of Christ was directed to our salvation, not least his road to Calvary.

The Way of the Cross was at first simply a revisiting of the holy places in the form of a pilgrimage. It was in the twelfth century that this crystallised as a contemplative form of prayer in the spirit of sharing in the sufferings of Christ. This has come down to us in the form of the fourteen stations we all know, but its development passed through many variations in the number and choice of incidents.

The Second Vatican Council, far from minimising the value of popular Christian 'pious exercises', wanted them accorded greater attention so as to link them more closely to the liturgical celebration of the salvation mystery: 'Popular devotions of the Christian people, provided they conform to the laws and norms of the Church, are to be highly recommended.... But such devotions should be so drawn up that they harmonise with the sacred liturgy' (SC 13).

It was in response to this directive that John Paul II, giving favourable consideration to experiments already made in various Christian communities, in 1991 adopted a new form for the Way of the Cross, one which adheres more closely to the Gospel narrative.

Renzo Agasso has adopted this latter series in presenting the following meditations on the Passion. They consist of short suggestive rhythmic phrases, mere sighs at times, including thoughts not put into words obviously, able to resonate in the soul and tune it in to Christ who still today cries out to us: 'I thirst', but then: 'Come to me, all you that are weary and are carrying heavy burdens, and I will give you rest' (Mt 11:29).

M.L.

•

Before each Station the following invocation may be said:
We adore you, O Christ, and we bless you.
Because by your holy cross you have redeemed the world.

After each meditation the Our Father is said.

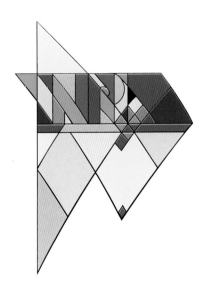

1

First Station

Jesus in the Garden of Olives

Jesus went out with his disciples to a place across the Kidron valley where there was a garden, and he went in with his disciples.
(From the Gospel according to John)

Darkness.
Gethsemane.
Soul sorrowful unto death.
Sweat. Blood.
Let this cup pass from me,
I do not want it.
Rebellion. Weakness of the flesh.
Heaven above mute.
God silent.
Does God stay silent?

2

Second Station

**Jesus, betrayed
by Judas, is arrested**

*Jesus said to him, "Judas, would you betray
the Son of Man with a kiss?"*

(From the Gospel according to Luke)

Judas is coming.
Swords and staves. The military.
Crowding around the just one.
A kiss. Do you betray me with a kiss?
Who are you Judas?
You did not understand.
Or maybe, yes. Who knows.
You wanted to be higher up.
A rope, the branch of a tree.
Below, thirty pieces of silver.

3

Third Station

Jesus is condemned by the Sanhedrin

They took Jesus to the high priest at whose house the chief priests and the elders and the scribes were gathered.

(From the Gospel according to Mark)

Masters of nothing.
Before them they have the Son of God.
Blind guides.
Somebody speaks up for him.
Nicodemus. Joseph of Arimathea.
It is not enough.
He must die. Why?
He is not one of us. How can they allow it?
The servant is standing there. Alone.
Surrounded by hatred.
Sent to the death of Death.

4

Fourth Station

**Jesus
is denied by Peter**

*"I do not know the man." At once the cock
crew; and Peter remembered how Jesus had
said: "Before the cock has crowed you will
deny me three times."*

(From the Gospel according to Matthew)

Peter, why?
You especially, the rock.
You ate with him. You have seen.
You, the fisher of men.
How could you say, and say again:
I do not know him.
Fear. Cowardice. No, no.
It seemed all was over.
Darkness, and men running away.
All over for ever.
Weep, Peter. You denied him three times.
A cock crowed for you.

5

Fifth Station

**Jesus
is judged by Pilate**

*Pilate said to the chief priests and the people:
"I do not find this man guilty of any crime."*
(From the Gospel according to Luke)

Behold the man. Before Pilate.
Who are you, Jesus?
Why are you disturbing the peace?
You know I can grant you life or death.
Truth. What is truth?
You say you are a king.
But we have a king.
Cruel and despotic.
You, sheep for the slaughter, what is it
    you want?
Leave us in peace.
And Pilate washes his hands.

6

Sixth Station

Jesus is scourged and crowned with thorns

They dressed him up in purple, and plaited a crown of thorns and put it on his head.
(From the Gospel according to Mark)

Flecks of blood on the flagstones
of the praetorium.
The soldiers mock.
A rag of purple.
Sharp thorns driven into the head.
Hail king of the Jews. King.
My kingdom is not of this world.
The whip cracks down on flesh.
Mute suffering. Coarse laughter. Spittle.
Poor Christ. King.
Stone steps for a throne. A crown
    of thorns.
Torn flesh.

7

Seventh Station

**Jesus
carries his cross**

So Jesus was given into their charge. He went out, carrying his own cross, to the place called in Hebrew 'Golgotha', that is, 'The place of the skull'.

(From the Gospel according to John)

Wood for the son of the carpenter.
Cross of infamy.
The way of sorrow. Shouting. Tears.
Soldiers and shopkeepers. Faces.
Shoulders bent. Get on.
Destination Golgotha.
The Place of the Skull.
Reserved to the condemned criminals.
Get on. Shameful procession.
Passing in front of all the houses.
All the shop fronts.
Women and children.
A man bearing a cross.

8

Jesus is helped to carry his cross

On the way out, they met a man named Simon from Cyrene, and forced him to carry his cross.

(From the Gospel according to Matthew)

Coming from the country, the man of
    Cyrene.
Had you ever met?
Forced to carry such a weight.
A look into each other's eyes.
Help me. Here I am.
Not passing by chance.
Wanted to see the good man.
Maybe not. It was he looking for you.
You in a million.
Why me, Lord? And the man bearing the
    cross says:
Why not you?

9

Ninth Station

**Jesus meets
the women of Jerusalem**

*Jesus turned to them and said: "Daughters
of Jerusalem, do not weep for me. Weep for
yourselves and for your children."*
(From the Gospel according to Luke)

Women's tears.
Veronica. More faces.
Weep not for me.
For your children.
Mothers. Like Mary.
Where is Mary?
Women's despair.
They have believed him,
followed his every step.
Now the road leads to Golgotha.
What will become of us?

10

Tenth Station

Jesus
is crucified

*When they came to the place called 'Calvary',
they crucified him there, with the criminals
one on his right hand and one on his left.*
(From the Gospel according to Luke)

Crucified. Lifted up
between heaven and earth.
The cry. The lance. The jar of vinegar.
Everything fulfilled.
Father, forgive them, they do not know.
Hostile shouts. The inscription:
    King of the Jews.
I will draw all to me.
Eli, Eli, lema sabachtani.
Night over Skull Hill.
The veil of the temple rent.
Reckoned among the evil-doers.

11

Jesus promises the Kingdom to the good thief

"Jesus, remember me when you come with your royal power!" Jesus replied: "I tell you truly, this very day you shall be with me in paradise."

(From the Gospel according to Luke)

You will be with me.
A thief all my life.
Redeemed by this man.
Who are you to take me with you?
Hung up. Like me.
Tell me. Why did they take you?
Torturing spasms.
Blasphemies. No, no.
It's right we should be here.
But him. He's not like us.
Wherever it is you're going, take me too.

12

Twelfth Station

Jesus on the cross, his mother, and the disciple

When Jesus saw his mother and the disciple whom he loved standing by her, he said to his mother: "Woman, there is your son."

(From the Gospel according to John)

Woman, your son.
Son, your mother.
All the children, all the mothers.
No one is alone any more.
Mary. John.
Begin again.
Away from Golgotha.
For the world.
If the grain of wheat does not die
it remains alone.
It bears fruit if it dies.

13

Thirteenth Station

Jesus
dies on the cross

Then Jesus cried in a loud voice: "Father, into your hands I entrust my spirit", and with these words he died.

(From the Gospel according to Luke)

I have said.
Lord, what did you say?
Away from me Satan.
No one has a greater love.
Love hung on the cross.
The last breath.
All is accomplished.
The cup. Let me drain it.
The heavens rent.
God is silent.
Is God really silent?

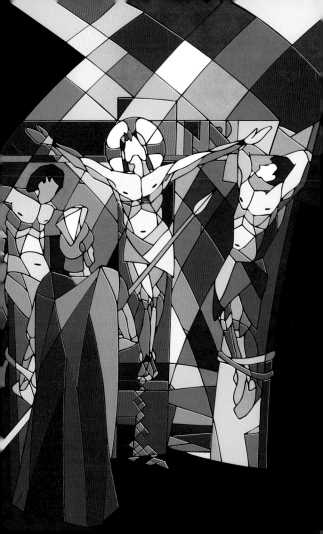

14 Fourteenth Station

Jesus is laid in the tomb

Joseph took the body of Jesus and wound it in a clean linen shroud, and laid it in a new tomb, which he had had cut out of a rock.

(From the Gospel according to Matthew)

A new rock tomb
hollowed out quite recently
for Joseph of Arimathea.
A good man. Give me his body.
Taking down from the cross. Ointments.
The white shroud.
God is dead?
The stone sealed.
Soldiers on guard. Fires in the night.
Silence. The end.
Doors barred. Fears.
All buried with him.

15

Fifteenth Station

The resurrection

Do not be amazed. You are looking for Jesus of Nazareth who was crucified. He has been raised up, he is not here. Look, there is the place where he was laid ! Go now, and say to Peter and the other disciples: "Jesus is going ahead of you into Galilee, and you will see him there, as he told you."

(From the Gospel according to Mark)

The third day.
The women come running.
Why do you look for him among the dead?
He lives. He is alive. Tell Peter.
Easter morning.
The joy, the beating heart.
He had said it.
We did not believe it.
Foolish and hard of heart.
I live for ever.
The stone rolled away.
I will be with you.

Prayers

The Sign of the Cross

In the name of the Father,
and of the Son,
and of the Holy Spirit, Amen.

The Lord's Prayer

Our Father,
who art in heaven,
hallowed be thy name;
thy kingdom come,
thy will be done on earth as it is in heaven.
Give us this day our daily bread;
and forgive us our trespasses
as we forgive those who trespass against us;
and lead us not into temptation,
but deliver us from evil. Amen.

The Hail Mary

Hail Mary, full of grace,
the Lord is with thee.
Blessed art thou among women,
and blessed is the fruit of thy womb, Jesus.
Holy Mary, Mother of God,
pray for us sinners,
now and at the hour of our death. Amen.

The Glory Be

Glory be to the Father,
   and to the Son,
      and to the Holy Spirit.
As it was in the beginning,
   is now, and ever shall be,
      world without end. Amen.

The Stabat Mater

Stabat Mater dolorosa
luxta crucem lacrimosa,
Dum pendebat Filius.

Cuius animam gementem,
Contristatam et dolentem
Pertransivit gladius.

O quam tristis et afflicta
Fuit illa benedicta
Mater unigeniti!

Quae maerebat et dolebat,
Pia Mater, dum videbat
Nati poenas incliti.

Quis est homo qui non fleret,
Matrem Christi si videret
In tanto supplicio?

Quis non potest contristari,
Christi Matrem contemplari
Dolentem cum Filio?

Pro peccatis suae gentis,
Vidit Iesum in tormentis,
Et flagellis subditum.

Vidit suum dulcem natum
Moriendo desoltum,
Dum emisit spiritum.

Eia Mater fons amoris,
Me sentire vim doloris
Fac, ut tecum lugeam.

Fac ut ardeat cor meum
In amando Christum Deum,
Ut sibi complaceam.

Sancta Mater, istud agas,
Crucifixi fige plagas
Cordi meo valide.

Tui nati vulnerati,
Tam dignati pro me pati,
Poenas mecum divide.

Fac me tecum pie flere,
Crucifixo condolere,
Donec ego vixero.

Iuxta crucem tecum stare,
Et me tibi sociare
In planctu desidero.

Virgo virginum praeclara,
Mihi iam non sis amara:
Fac me tecum plangere.

Fac ut portem Christi mortem
Passionis fac consortem,
Et plagas recolere.

Fac me plagis vulnerari,
Fac me cruce inebriari,
Et cruore Filii.

Flammis ne urar succensus,
Per te, virgo, sim defensus
In die iudicii.

Christe, cum sit hinc exire,
Da per Matrem me venire
Ad palmam victoriae.

Quando corpus morietur,
Fac ut animae donetur
Paradisi gloria.

* * *

At the cross her station keeping,
stood the mournful mother weeping,
close to Jesus to the last.

Through her heart, his sorrow sharing,
all his better anguish bearing,
now at length the sword has passed.

Oh, how sad and sore distressed
was that mother highly blest,
of the sole-begotten One.

Christ above in torment hangs;
she beneath beholds the pangs
of her dying glorious Son.

Is there one who would not weep,
whelm'd in miseries so deep,
Christ's dear mother to behold?

Can the human heart refrain
from partaking in her pain,
in that mother's pain untold?

Bruised, derided, cursed, defiled,
she beheld her tender child,
all with bloody scourges rent;

For the sins of his own nation,
saw him hang in desolation,
till his spirit forth he sent.

O thou mother! Fount of love!
Touch my spirit from above,
make my heart with thine accord:

Make feel as thou hast felt;
make my soul to glow and melt
with the love of Christ my Lord.

Holy mother, pierce me through,
in my heart each wound renew
of my Saviour crucified.

Let me share with thee his pain
who for all my sins was slain,
who for me in torments died.

Let me mingle tears with thee,
mourning him who mourned for me,
all the days that I may live:

By the cross with thee to stay,
there with thee to weep and pray,
is all I ask of thee to give.